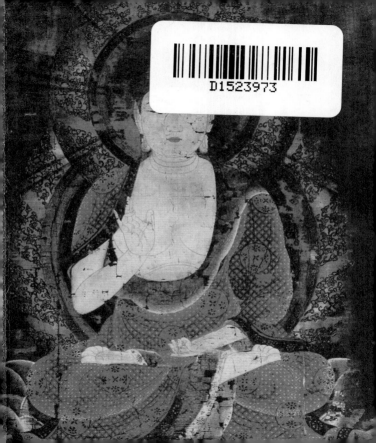

ZEN wisdom

by Daniel Abdal-Hayy Moore

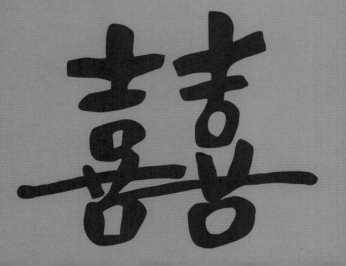

ISBN: 1-933662-02-6

This book may be ordered by mail from the publisher.
Please include $3.50 for postage and handling.

Please support your local bookseller first!

Books published by Cider Mill Press Book Publishers are available
at special discounts for bulk purchases in the United States
by corporations, institutions, and other organizations.
For more information, please contact the publisher.

Cider Mill Press Book Publishers
"Where good books are ready for press"
12 Port Farm Road
Kennebunkport, Maine 04046

Visit us on the web!
www.cidermillpress.com

Design by: Julie Reynolds, Lana Mullen, and Melany Kuhn
Typography: Astoria Titling and Franklin Gothic

Printed in China
1 2 3 4 5 6 7 8 9 0
First Edition

Contents

ZEN + ZEN = ZEN:
Is That a Rooster Crowing?

I salute my two teachers in this enterprise: Zen Master Shunryu Suzuki Roshi and Sufi Master Baji Tayyaba Khanum, but where one ends and the other begins, I cannot tell.

BUDDHA NATURE

Pointing directly to the human mind;
Seeing into one's nature, one becomes a Buddha.

Bodhidharma

Zen is the rock we must transform into air, the brick we need to polish into a clear, reflecting mirror, the heart of us we need to open and expand, our mind we need to still and make tranquil, thus tasting eternity—the reality of our mortal existence from birth to death and beyond. Zen is the Path to liberation from the wheel of suffering into the light of Buddha nature, taken literally. It is not words, nor books, nor even Masters and traditions—it is experience. But it is not even experience. And, of course, it is not even *not* experience. Ha! Now I've taken the bull by the horns …and painted myself into a typical Zen corner!

Bodhidharma (AD fifth-sixth centuries), seen as the founder of what would flower into Zen practice and direct face-to-face confrontation with one's original nature, seems to be one of those outrageously radical beings who appear among us from time to time to shock us into taking our "religion" seriously and achieve the original goal of all religions: *enlightenment*. In Sufism, the famous Master of the Persian mystical poet Rumi, Shams of Tabriz, was an uncompromising but wildly wise companion and teacher, like Bodhidharma, who brought Rumi to heights of poetic ecstasy and humanitarian compassion. These spiritual giants appear on the scene, topple suppositions, challenge sclerotic authorities and mummified scholars, ignite hearts and blow minds, and then move on, leaving a legacy of Light.

Japanese Zen *sumi-e* brush paintings, in swashes of black ink on rice paper scrolls, often show a scowling, craggy, hunched kind of character as Bodhidharma, and the legendary story of his encounters, first with authority and much later with a disciple, have the rough-hewn quality of no-holds-barred but intuitively penetrating wisdom.

The Emperor Wu-ti of the Lian Dynasty asked him, "Since I am building monasteries and supporting monks, what merit will I gain?" Bodhidharma answered (and we can imagine he did so without blinking), "No merit." Was that hissing sound we just heard the sudden intake of breath from his court eunuchs? Bodhidharma then went on to explain that this was because the Emperor's motives were impure. The astounded Emperor then asked what true merit was. Bodhidharma answered, "It is pure knowing, wonderful and perfect. Its essence is emptiness. One cannot gain such merit by worldly means."

It is said that the emperor didn't quite grasp this answer, no doubt taking it simply at face value, and Bodhidharma moved on in his travels, though he may have found it expedient to do so. This and no doubt other experiences convinced him to spread Buddhist Realism, the experiential essence of Buddha's teaching. So for nine years, Bodhidharma sat in meditation in a remote monastic cave, facing the wall of a high cliff known as Shoshitsu Mountain, cut off from everyone, day and night, cross-legged, in imitation of the Buddha's own practice.

In the Zen paintings, he appears to almost become the very rock-face itself, so determined is he. But in the end, his mind was clear, pure as empty sky illumined by a full moon, while elsewhere busy monks in

monastery halls argued and puzzled over obtuse points of Buddhist doctrine.

Then one day a student named Eka made the arduous journey to Bodhidharma's cave to ask him for the true teachings of the Way. Bodhidharma remained silent, so Eka left, returning three years later to stand patiently outside his cave entrance, all night, in the dead of winter. Some accounts have it that Eka even cut off his own left arm and presented it to the Master to prove his sincerity, though there are commentators who say it is only a metaphor to express Eka's total rejection of every other previous method for reaching the truth. In any case (in one of those Shams/Rumi moments), Bodhidharma finally broke his silence. He asked Eka (in a roar, in a whisper?), "Well, what do you want?" By now Eka is fluff waiting to be blown on a wind, hanging like a dis-interred root from the edge of a cliff, as fine as an ant's antenna feeling its way forward, and literally up to his waist in snow, armless or not, focused on his question in a way we cannot imagine from our everyday lives. Finally Eka replied, "My mind is not at peace. How can it be pacified?" Bodhidharma answered, "Bring it to me and I will pacify it!" Eka replied, "It is impossible to bring you my mind!" Bodhidharma said, "*There!* I have pacified it."

Eka understood. He burst through dualistic thinking, soared past interpretations of the Buddha's teachings, and instantaneously experienced the *satori* we've heard so much about. And yet, curiously, after the *satori* experience, in which somehow the mind either reconciles dualities or bursts through them like a lightning bolt—living permanently on the other side of the conflict—even the former "rule-bound" patterns of the world now make divine sense. One has a true *in-seeing* to the essence of all things and finds perfect harmony.

- Before Zen training mountains are mountains and rivers are rivers.
- During Zen training mountains are no longer mountains and rivers are no longer rivers.
- After Zen training, mountains are mountains and rivers are rivers.

Consider this little book as a shiny pebble you might find on the road where you usually take a stroll; it catches your eye by its small, unusual gleam. As you turn it in the light, it occurs to your mind that it might even be a precious stone! But if it turns out to be a bit of mica or schist after all, and it still stands out to your eye, you pick it up and put it in your pocket.

This book in relation to the actual practice of Zen is like that. Zen has a long and noble history, the core experiential teachings of Buddhism, passed from enlightened Master to Master, rigorous in its training and majestic in its doctrine, century after century. It goes further than Buddhism as "religion," in that the training of Zen is a process of finally (but one might also say *initially*) experiencing what the Buddha experienced in his *satori*, his burst of wisdom. Who then, rather than simply becoming a venerable, wise hermit in a cave of eternal silence, was prophetically "sent" among us to explain the doctrine revealed to him, out of compassion for humankind, and to lay down for all time the method of reaching his actual state of liberation and enlightenment, open to every sentient being: *ourselves*.

But Zen has developed paradoxically, perhaps more so than any spiritual Path, with deep though unhistorically direct connections to Judaic Hasidism and Islamic Sufism, as well as the paradoxes of some great Christian mystics, such as Meister Eckhart, or the poets John Donne or William Blake. It is the espousal of the natural mind, of our true natures, of our original Face, of our being in its totality and its oneness, in its whole-

ness, in its Buddha nature. But actual realization of it may only be released from its shell by a crash of conundrum, a head-banging, heart-wrenching mind-twister that finally, like the Gordian knot, falls apart at the touch of the sword of Zen.

Zen Buddhists experience light. The Zen experience *itself* is light. Unless, of course, it is dark ...then the Zen experience is darkness. One might say that the Zen experience is experience itself, whatever comes, faced with perfect composure. Contemporary Zen Master Sensei Suzuki, has said, "We can enjoy our life only with our limited body. Without limitation nothing exists. So we should enjoy our limitations." We should strive to reach what has always been with us—our True Nature. It seems that way for all of us, doesn't it? Unless we get so sidetracked and waylaid that we lose sight of any soulful center, in which case we probably wouldn't have picked up this pebble book to begin with! (Nor I have written it ...)

But this book isn't the thing itself, it isn't Zen, and by reading it you may not attain any Zen perspective. On the other hand, Zen is such that you already have the enlightenment within you, not in some giddy new-age way, but in a very ancient, realized way in the very essence of your humanity, by your simple fact of being born. Other "ways" might call it a "soul," or "consciousness," but in Zen it is called "Buddha nature"—our original nature. The very wisdom we were born with.

What happened to it? Where did it go after all? Why is there a nostalgia for it that makes us wish to regain it? How many multitudes of seekers have felt and longed for the same thing? Zen monasteries with straight-backed disciples sitting day after day, working at simple physical tasks, pounding rice, studying difficult treatises, having strong and often enigmatic face-to-face interviews with their Masters?

The original Buddha nature of the Universe—call it the *Void*, call it *Brahma*, call it *Allah* or *God*—sent the Buddha (and all the other prophets), and all the Buddhist sages, time after time to arrive at the threshold of our normal consciousness, to set out on the journey to greater knowledge and greater peace. This has always been the same, in every era, in every culture. A recent *New Yorker* cartoon shows a Neanderthal man and woman, primitive in their skins and with shaggy hair, the man holding a club, the woman saying, "I don't know if I want to bring a baby into this crazy world ..."

If one rock found on the road can lead to a path of wisdom, why is it that so many other rocks lead nowhere? Why is it that one rock out of all the rocks available to us somehow emanates a magnetism of seeking? Why were we put on earth to be faced with such conundrums? How is it that some mortal humans like ourselves in almost all respects but one paramount one (some innate, divine luminous wisdom and a truly humble but superhuman confidence) are sent with a Path and a "scripture" or science of living in perfection, with layers and levels of accomplishment? Who sends them? What amazing tumblers of the cosmic safe's secret combination lock fall into place to present us with this saint or that sage who compassionately takes us by the heart to lift us out of the deep wells of our individuality? Puts us on dry land again. Dry, dry land. Dries us out. To our essential cores?

What is our original face, from before we were born? The Soto Zen teacher emphasizes this over and over. Our original face ...not this one with its nose and lips and blemishes and wink of eye. A face that may be the eternal and divine face from the depths of our origin whose supersonic glance brought our hearts to life in the first place!

Some Definitions As We Carry On

Awakening: Enlightenment. Bringing sentient beings across the ocean of birth and death to the shore of enlightenment, or saving sentient beings.

Bodhidharma: He brought Zen teaching from India to China and is regarded as the twenty-eighth Indian Ancestor and the First Chinese Ancestor. According to legend, he sat facing the wall in Zazen for nine years at Shaolin Monastery.

Buddha nature: The capacity for becoming a Buddha, which is inherent in all sentient beings according to Mahayana Buddhist teaching. It has never been lost and can be experienced through the continuous practice of Zen.

Dharma: Ultimate law, reality, or truth. Teaching of truth, all things, or phenomena.

Koan: A fundamental point, first principle, truth that is experienced directly. An exemplary story pointing to this realization. Zen riddles that can be understood only by bypassing the rational mind.

Nirvana: The state of enlightenment attained by Shakyamuni Buddha, or by any Buddha. Literally, "extinction of fire," meaning extinction of desires, or liberation from the cycle of birth, death, and rebirth.

Satori: The experience of awakening, which comes from the Japanese word *satoru*, "to know." It occurs when dualistic views are no longer obscuring reality.

Shakyamuni Buddha: The founding teacher of Buddhism who lived in India around the fifth century, B.C. In the Mahayana Buddhist tradition, his enlightenment as the awakening of all sentient beings is emphasized.

Splish-Splash:
The Art of Zen Brush Painting

Everything that has true depth also has a certain wild spontaneity. Things take place in time in an odd way, coming into our scope to hang almost—but not quite—suspended: occurrences, objects, brushes with life or death; and then they uncannily seem to either move "forward" with us, or wisp away. The Zen Masters (and the true masters of all revealed paths) seem to share both a monumental solidity within their spiritual realm, almost mountainous, as well as a delicacy that seems most ephemeral in its relation to time (the Buddha simply raises a flower to transmit The Way). These very human but extraordinary folk seem most eternal when they are most *in the moment*. And this is our experience also, whenever it happens to blessedly occur to us, that the most monumental moments are like English poet Robert Browning's lines:

That's the wise thrush; he sings each song
   twice over

Lest you should think he never could recapture
The first fine careless rapture! ...

The first fine careless rapture! That's the eternal moment whose time enters and exits from a single point simultaneously.

Dogen (1200–1253, among the first to transmit Zen from China to Japan, founder of the Soto school of Zen) says: "You may suppose that time is only passing away and not understand that time never arrives. Although understanding itself is time, understanding does not depend on its own arrival. People only see time's coming and going, and do not thoroughly understand that 'time-being,' or 'present time,' abides in each moment."

Now, the Masters have neither jettisoned everything but the present moment, nor kept anything in their compass *but* the present moment. Dogen has defined "time-being" as the only time, since the "past" is what has "gone from" the moment and the "future" is what is "coming into" the moment. However, both have no reality unto themselves except in their relation to the present moment, which, in some way, never arrives. We really live consistently outward from the moment in which we find ourselves, from birth to death. Our True Nature is in this *understanding*, since nothing is perfect in either the present nor in the past. It is only in the present that perfection can be found.

Recognizing this, the Soto school of Zen emphasizes the practice of Zazen meditation itself, focusing on the moment, whatever it is, both in the meditation hall in protracted sessions of strict sitting, or in the world of hustle-bustle and conflict, chopping wood, carrying water, visiting the doctor, bringing up children, fighting the school board …dying. All are part of the practice, and in that they are also all part of the Buddha. The practice is the thing, *in which to catch the conscience of the King* ...Buddha is not a figure from the past to whom we must aspire, nor a perfect state in the future unto which we should lovingly long, but will never quite reach. Already enlightened, by conscientious and assiduous practice, we may become "re-enlightened." But there is still a paradox here (going *toward* enlightenment, *already* enlightened) inherent in the practice itself. Which never ends.

How does one give living expression to this recognition? We see a perfect paradigm of this in the long and glorious tradition of Zen ink-painting, or *sumi-e*, instantaneous swashes of brushed black ink on rice-paper scrolls, normally just black on white, and centuries later just as fresh as when the ink was drying after the virgin moment of its virgin application. Everything counts on the wielded performance of the stroke, brush loaded, and on the poised and "carelessly rapturous" or "enrapturedly careless" state of

the brush wielder. The character and spiritual power of the Master, monk, or nun is telegraphed instantly into the painting by the free concentration of the artist at the time the brush swashes, each stroke as perfect as possible at the moment of its perfection. This spiritual quality is called, in Japanese, *bokki*. These are paintings entered into not just with our sight, but intuitively, in a dimension far greater really than mere black image on white scroll, putting us into the same moment of intellect, feeling, experience, and its ingenious summation, that "eternally momentary" state in which the artist was at the peak of his or her ecstatic inspiration.

A circle that could be a nebula, quick black circumference surrounding nothing but light, a picture of grim Bodhidharma scowling in his cave, tough as rock, birds on a branch, flowers on a bush, feathery sky with a few feathery clouds, Japanese or Chinese proverbs, *koans* or nonsense phrases written like waterfalls or shimmering with heat or light (often inscrutable even to those who are able to read those languages). These words and images shimmer on the paper as if they haven't even been painted, but just evoked out of the cross-laid rice fibers of the paper itself. Ephemeral and momentous at the same time. Exactly the same as their living onlookers, mirror contemplating a mirror.

The circle is the Zen symbol "supreme," known as an *enso*, representing (or even actually being) a circle of enlightenment. Zen has sometimes been defined as, "A circle like vast space, nothing missing, nothing extra," an inscription that often accompanies the *sumi-e* ink painting of the *enso* circle itself. Some lines from the poem, "The World," by the seventeenth-century English poet Henry Vaughan evokes this circular illumination:

I saw Eternity the other night,
Like a great ring of pure and endless light,

All calm, as it was bright;
And round beneath it, Time in hours,
   days, years,
Driv'n by the spheres
Like a vast shadow mov'd; in which the world
And all her train were hurl'd.

What we notice about the Zen circles as they whip by us, sometimes in a hurry to disappear altogether, sometimes asserting their utter solidity, is that while each is a circle, each is also distinct, even by the same artist. Some are perfectly symmetrical, almost machinelike in their circularity; others are completely lopsided. Some may be one continuous and sinuous brushstroke; some two energetic attempts making perfection. One circle might faintly resemble a snake biting its tail, the famed and fabled Uroboros; another sits there like a rice cake, brazenly material, waiting to be eaten? Another might be a wisp of the faintest thread of a circle, as if on an exhalation of breath;

another like a stone wheel rolling into the air. On and on these brash or wispy circles seem to go, into a bubbling infinity of thick and thin circumferences, each evoking both their own somethingness and their essential emptiness, a basic articulation, however faint, and ineffable silence, a moment in time as well as endlessness—in a perfectly controlled round splash: *enlightenment*.

The circle as such a powerful image of the imageless may go back to a typical Zen encounter between master and disciple, in this case a monk and his Master Isan. The monk asked his Master for a *gatha* (a spiritual representation) of enlightenment. Master Isan characteristically refused, saying, "It is right in front of your face! Why should I express it in brush and ink?" But undaunted, the intrepid monk went on to ask Kyozan, another master, for the same thing. Kyozan conceded, drew a circle on a piece of paper, and then added, as if both encircling and *un*-circling

his sparkling and startling new circle: "Thinking about this and then understanding it is second best; not thinking about it and understanding it is third best." But, of course, he didn't say what *first best* was.

The primary types of *enso* are:

1. Mirror *enso*—A simple circle free of any accompanying inscription that leaves everything to the insight of the viewer.

2. Universe *enso*—A circle that represents the cosmos (similar to the curved space of modern physics?).

3. Moon *enso*—The full moon, clear and bright, that silently illuminates all beings without discrimination.

4. Zero *enso*—Time and space are "empty," but they give birth to the fullness of existence.

5. Wheel *enso*—All life, subject to change, revolves in circles.

6. Sweet-cake *enso*—When enlightenment and the acts of daily life—"sipping tea and eating rice cakes"—are one, there is true Buddhism.

7. "What is this?" *enso*—The most frequently used inscription on Zen circle paintings, which says, "Discover the meaning for yourself!"

But Zen brush paintings depict other subjects besides circles, occasionally leaving those evocatively Spartan representations of enlightenment to paint whimsical figures of Bodhidharma (or *Daruma*, the Japanese name derived from the Sanskrit word "dharma"), monks in almost comical processions, or finely evoked flowers on branches, birds in a bush, buckets filling with rain. But these paintings are always executed with an intense economy of means, and always as a tellingly deep expression of the original nature of the painter. It is recognized that a painting of Daruma, besides being a symbol of Bodhidharma's penetrating insight, powerful will, ceaseless diligence, and fierce rejection of all externals, is really a self-portrait of the artist at the other end of the brush. The artist to paint Daruma must become Daruma, somehow embodying both Daruma's cragginess of effort as well as the enlightened effortlessness of Zen practice.

Calligraphy, as in Islam, is also most common among the Zen *sumi-e* painters. *Ichigyo sho*, or "one-line calligraphies," are poetic phrases or Zen sayings usually consisting of five to seven characters written vertically on a hanging scroll. The next most popular theme for Zen calligraphers is *ichijikan*, "one-word barriers," a single, large character brushed as a visual *koan*, a brain-teasing spiritual conundrum that obliterates illusion. The single, imposing character—for example, *MU* (nothingness), *ICHI* (one), *KAN* (barrier)—either stands on its own or has an accompanying inscription written in smaller characters to explain its meaning. But these Chinese or Japanese characters, gorgeously painted but often inscrutable, even while asserting lightning-like liveliness, dance on a usually horizontal scroll with an almost dervish energy. And, in fact, these Zen calligraphies are similar to many calligraphed inscriptions in Arabic, either in ancient Kufic or more modern letters, which entwine around themselves with their loops, ascenders, and descenders as if alive, and yet are often nearly impossible to read even by Arabs, while still fully articulating their own distinctive spiritual voice.

Rinzai and Soto Zen artists typically quote from sutras or the sayings of a Master, but Zen Masters and Zen monk artists will paint nearly anything. In fact, the absolute *anythingness* of things is what is closest to their hearts, with examples including an

abbot defecating in a field or a Zen bicycle. Mount Fuji is always a popular subject, as a towering yet serene symbol of non-duality, but so are pine trees, bamboo stalks and plum blossoms, along with fancier orchids and chrysanthemums. And even then, Zen masters, monks, and nuns like to paint them as aspects of Buddha nature rather than simply as pretty plants and flowers. It's when things are seeming to enjoy their simple being, be they rocks or wood or living things, animal or human, seated deeply within their uniqueness but without any pretensions whatsoever, that they might appear in a Zen brush painting. They call out in their silence throughout eternity that Buddha nature is, well ...*everything that is*, manifested in the similarly unique and living brushstroke, both alive and not alive, here and not here, both wispily evanescent and as tough and durable as the ink of the paintings themselves, soot made of burnt pine and lamp black mixed with glue and camphor ...

EAST MEETS WEST:
Dripping Water, Slamming Doors

It may be said that the true activity of Zen practice (and really that of all spiritual Paths) is the often difficult and strangely enigmatic integration of our inner and outer beings. Whether we call our inner and outer beings soul and body, thought and action, or even pacifist/activist, we may be isolating the crucial difference between maintaining an elegant poise in our lives as against a sad, slow-motion collapse. How do we go through this life we've been kerplunked into, like it or not? Do we make constant missteps, bungles, even tragic mistakes, or are we in a fairly steady state of serene harmony (with occasional outbursts of necessary *explosive* harmony), vital and present to the very end of our lives, fully meeting and mirroring the requirements of every moment?

But this integration also includes an expansion of our inner and outer beings, often way beyond our expectations, dilating them both as widely as possible to vast

46

inner worlds where all of time's wisdom simultaneously exists, as well as to more compassionately
effective outer worlds, where through even one subtle
gesture we might help other living beings reach their
enlightenment. As Walt Whitman says in his epic *Song
of Myself*:

> Do I contradict myself?
> Very well then.... I contradict myself;
> I am large.... I contain multitudes.

Zen takes us to the extreme brittle edges of our inner
being, say, to see the plain fact of our outer being
more clearly, or, vice-versa, takes us to the limits of
our outer being to see the unsuspected richness of
our inner resources, then blows the duality up completely once and for all. The paradox here, as Zen
Master Sensei Suzuki so often repeated, is that by
truly embracing our *limitations* we find Buddha
nature—by accepting our limits, in human form and

mysterious soul-creation, we find they've been replaced by a generous allotment from The Unlimited. Then the ego-shattered, ego-surrendered, limitation-aware devotee knows what to do in any given situation, acting confidently from an integrated center. But the center then becomes not our own tight little personal knottiness of selfhood, but the divinely designed pattern of the cosmic "self," alive and well from before our birth, which sees farther and speaks from deeper than we could ever imagine from our affable but admittedly peculiar personality. At some great zenith point it may not be "our" center at all, but that of universal Buddha nature, or of God's now no longer mysterious Presence (and Sensei Suzuki spoke of God in this way), now acting from Big Mind, rather than Small Mind.

We seem to have entered the Age of Explosions. Sad to say, this is literally true, with terrorists misrepresenting various political grievances all over the world by resorting to body-bursting and heart-rending bombings to make their point. But it is equally true that we have an explosion of media and miraculously streamlined technology bringing more "knowledge" and more information to our fingertips, even about spirituality. The fact that we can send and receive e-mails instantly around the globe from a little handheld machine is an astonishing detonation whose impact has changed the sentient texture of our world. So far, we are still more or less able to distinguish between virtual and non-virtual reality—but the time may be getting short. There appears to be a serious disconnect between blithely oblivious populations consuming material goods and tragically prosecuted billion-dollar, casualty-chaotic wars in distant lands, with no strong resistance to their injustice on the part of the people footing the bill, both physically and financially.

Urgent feelings of time shortening and quickening for us, and our need for a hold on eternity in our momen-

tary experience, makes us begin to search for a time-tested and true Path to more awareness of our world based not on newspaper headlines, but on the fall of a leaf, the soft whisper of snow, the very air in the room, the heartbeat in our bodies, the unseen spectacle of Paradise—earthly or heavenly—that lies just behind the visible and experienced reality of every day.

We also know that with an established center of peace within us, we would be able to see more clearly into the hearts of those who are *not* ourselves. Being *au courant* these days is to be globally aware, and the prayer is that each of us becomes an awakened element in an all-encompassing planetary soul that seeks peace and enlightenment, echoing and reasserting the Buddhist vow to save all sentient beings before we ourselves enter the Nirvana of perfect bliss.

(At the same time that everything comes, literally, to our fingertips, it is necessary to emphasize that to truly advance along the Path of Zen Buddhism, it is best to find a bona fide Zen Master in our locality and put ourselves under his or her mastery, the effect of which no amount of book reading can possibly duplicate.

I sat with a true and great Zen master in the early 1960s in San Francisco, Sensei Shunryu Suzuki, of the Soto Zen School, which emphasizes re-enlightenment from our original natures by simply sitting quietly in Zazen meditation and watching our thoughts go back and forth to no purpose and letting them go, detaching and releasing our thoughts and anxieties to swim by and out of our line of vision. And he was this perfectly poised person always on the brink of some mild revelation, which might bring about a very dulcet laughter from somewhere both deep and human within him or a profoundly thoughtful inner contemplation accompanied by an almost olfactory sweetness. He was the example before us of a true human being, aware of his limitations, but whose realized well of inspiration was far deeper than any of our own.

Zen, like all the great mystical paths (Zen is the kernel of the kernel of Buddhism, what the Buddha himself, peace be upon him, gained in realization from his efforts and his submissive humility before the Greater Mind), can both be taught and cannot be taught. It has to be experienced. It is not words, yet it is often transmitted through words. That is the hope of this little book, that a spark might be ignited, and a reminder posted in our world to go into the placid center of ourselves where so much light is shedding itself constantly. Shedding itself! Throughout our original nature. Our Buddha nature.

Zen pits us face to face with a blank wall, and there's no escape. It hems us in; it confronts us with our nothingness in order to bring us to a point of annihilation, so that we can appreciate the true "somethingness" of our existence. But even this isn't true. We're trapped. It traps us and hems us in, so there's no left or right, up or down, forward or backward where we can go and be safe.

Most people, when they think of Zen, probably think of huge Zen monasteries with polished mahogany floors and Japanese woven tatami matting, incense wafting through the air, pretty flower arrangements or gardens with a soft tinkling of water down a bamboo tube into a wooden tub—something very serene and timeless. What most don't realize is that Zen is usually sitting for long—endlessly long—stretches of time, legs crossed uncomfortably (especially for Westerners used to chairs), facing a wall, watching the inevitable inhalation and exhalation of breath, sitting ramrod straight, hands in a fixed position, eyes half-closed and focused neither too far in nor too far out, letting thoughts come and go, however simple or however traumatic, back and forth, surging up and

dissipating, watching the breath, feeling the legs go numb, the hands want to relax, the back to slump, to give up, get up and leave, stay sitting, stay endlessly and rocklike sitting, with no particular joy nor excitement, that white light in the mind perhaps expanding a little, the breath becoming a bit deeper and the connection with breath and thoughts becoming a bit more unified ...But in this position, having made this commitment, we're trapped. And what smart thing can we say to the Master to show how really enlightened we are? What lovely retort to his nonsense or his wise question? How shall we show how really advanced we are after all, or if we don't think this, how horribly behind everyone else we are, with little hope of catching up.

Zen is a bitch. It's not all flower arrangements and incense through the meditation hall. It's a hard confrontation with the most essential aspect of being born—our mortality, our natures, our selfhood, our egos, our very "our-ness"—of which we are generally so proud and of which we are so protective.

Does Zen rip all of this away? And if it does, what are we left with? A cult mentality? But there's no Zen and no ripping away. Zen Masters often say this: There's nothing to attain, but unless we strive there's no attainment. Why not just take a walk in a forest and look lovingly at the trees and leaves, moths and squirrels, noting the mosses and stones? Isn't this enough? Glad to be alive? Isn't a genial appreciation and awakening perceptiveness enough? Watch the ants move along in their daily labors and the wasps buzz from their nests? Watch leaves fall?

In 1964, the year of long hair and patchouli oil, I was married in the San Francisco Zen Center by Shunryu Suzuki, the great Soto Zen Master. I was told that since I had no money, I should give him a gift of some kind for performing the ceremony.

Outside in a woodpile by my house, I found the door to a cabinet that had a beveled inset. I decided to write out one of my poems, decorate it with water-color, and paste it to the panel as a gift. I saw that there were some cocoons and old spider webs in the corners. "How Zen," I thought. "Suzuki will love this. I'll leave them there."

I wrapped it up in paper and took it to the Zen Center. Sensei Suzuki and his wife sat at a table outside his kitchen, and he accepted the gift. He opened it very carefully, took it in his very sensitive and rather deli-cate hands, and admiringly said, "Oh, this is very nice ...very, very nice." I was really happy. Then he got up from the table and took it into the kitchen with him. He was not gone long, when he emerged again with a cloth in his hand. He put the panel on the table and cleaned off all the cocoons and cobwebs. "That's better," he said. Then he thanked me.

Direct transmission through practice. I'm pondering that moment even now, forty years later.

So what is our mortality after all? From birth to death we're obligated to, well, eat, excrete, earn a living, take care of our bodies and the beings of others ...the list of obligations is rather endless. Buddhism, like all the great revelations, confronts any indifference we may have about our lives and brings us a revealed, "scientifically proven" (over many centuries) Path to openness and spiritual fulfillment, but not without an equally enormous effort to really pay attention, and pay some dues as well.

Try sitting very still for a few moments and concentrating simply on breath and nagging thoughts—emptying the mind, as they say, and not following any of thought's endless trains. It's not easy, and it's not really that pleasant. It isn't instantaneous enlightenment (though, in fact, it is). It may even feel a little claustrophobic. But with a bit more effort it becomes natural, then habitual, then nourishing, then centering, then the center of the universe—then nothing at all.

One time a monk met with Zen Master, Joshu. "O Master, I have just entered the monastery," he said. "Please teach me."

Joshu said, "Have you had your breakfast?"

"Yes, I have," answered the monk.

"Then," said Joshu, "wash your bowl."

Mindfulness in our daily life. Mindfulness in our practice. Washing out our own bowls and leaving no traces. Treading lightly on the earth and removing obstacles from the road, literally and figuratively. Helping others, whether they're mindful or not, grateful or not. Not expecting anything in return for all our efforts. Remaining poised in the worst of circumstances. Not getting angry (of utmost importance). In fact, squelching our anger. Not expressing everything our usual way, but in other more pleasing ways. Enjoying our limitations. Presenting ourselves fully within the moment itself, every moment itself. Living. Dying. Carrying on carrying on. Not saying. *Being*.

Continuous practice. *Zen*.

Zen Proverbs:
What They Said and
What They Did Not Say

*When you practice Zen you become one with Zen.
There is no you and no zazen. When you bow, there
is no Buddha and no you. One complete bowing takes
place, that is all. This is Nirvana.*

Shunryu Suzuki

*All Buddhas continuously abide in it, but do not leave
traces of consciousness in their illumination.
Sentient beings continuously move about in it, but
illumination is not manifest in their consciousness.*

Master Dogen

*Time present and time past
Are both perhaps present in time future,
And time future contained in time past.
If all time is eternally present
All time is unredeemable.*

T.S. Eliot, Four Quartets

You should arouse the thought of enlightenment. The thought of enlightenment has many names but they all refer to one and the same mind.

Ancestor Ngarjuna said, "The mind that fully sees into the uncertain world of birth and death is called the thought of enlightenment."

Thus if we maintain this mind, this mind can become the thought of enlightenment.

Master Dogen

To practice Zen one must be like a thief in the night, infiltrating without changing a thing. It is like dropping a pebble into a lake without raising a ripple.

Albert Low

Although its light is wide and great,
the moon is reflected
even in a puddle an inch wide.

Master Dogen

Whether talking or remaining silent,
Whether moving or standing quiet,
The Essence itself is ever at ease.

Daishi

Calm in quietude is not real calm.
When you can be calm in the midst of activity,
This is the true state of nature.

Huanchu Daoren

Do not seek the truth. Only cease to cherish opinions.
Zen Saying

One who excels in traveling leaves no wheel tracks.
Zen Tradition

Nothing is worth more than this day.

Johann Wolfgang von Goethe

We are here and it is now. Further than that, all human knowledge is moonshine.

H.L. Mencken

Sit. Rest. Work.
Alone with yourself, never weary.
On the edge of the forest live joyfully, without desire.

Buddha

We bow to Buddha because there is no Buddha.
If we bow to Buddha because there is Buddha,
that is not the right understanding.

Shunryu Suzuki Roshi

There is no place in Buddhism for using effort.
Just be ordinary and nothing special.

Lin-Chi

There are two ways to live your life. One is as though nothing is a miracle. The other is as though everything is a miracle.

Albert Einstein

There are no mundane things outside of Buddhism, and there is no Buddhism outside of mundane things.

Yuan-Wu

The miracle is not to fly in the air, or to walk on the water, but to walk on the earth.

Chinese Proverb

I drink tea and forget the world's noises.

Chinese Saying

Arranging a bowl of flowers in the morning can give a sense of quiet to a crowded day—like writing a poem or saying a prayer. What matters is that one be for a time inwardly attentive.

Ann Morrow Lindbergh

Realization, neither general nor particular, is effort without desire.

Master Dogen

The quieter you become the more you are able to hear.

Zen Saying

There is a silence into which the world cannot intrude. There an ancient peace you carry in your heart and have not lost.

A Course in Miracles

Meditating deeply ...reach the depth of the source. Branching streams cannot compare to this source! Sitting along in the great silence, even though the heavens turn and the earth is upset, you will not even wink.

Nyogen Senzaki

You do not need to leave your room. Remain sitting at your table and listen. Do not even listen, simply wait. Do not even wait, be still and solitary. The world will freely offer itself to you to be unmasked, it has no choice. It will roll in ecstasy at your feet.

Franz Kafka

Praying is not about asking; it's about listening ...It is just opening your eyes to see what was there all along.

Chagdud Tulku Rinpoche

The real voyage of discover consists not in seeking new landscapes but in having new eyes.

Marcel Proust

*Like the little stream
making its way through mossy crevices,
I, too, quietly, turn clear and transparent.*

Ryokan

It is as if a raindrop fell from heaven into a stream or fountain and became one with the water in it so that never again can the raindrop be separated from the water of the stream, or as if a little brook ran into the

sea and there was thenceforward no means of distin-
guishing its water from the ocean; or as if a brilliant
light came into a room through two windows and
though it comes in divided between them, it forms a
single light inside.

St. Teresa

Where beauty is, then there is ugliness;
where right is, also there is wrong.

Ryokan

Sentient beings are by nature Buddhas.
It is like water and ice.
There is no ice without water.
There are no Buddha's outside of sentient beings.

Hakuin

You wander from room to room
hunting for the diamond necklace
that is already around your neck!

Rumi

There is no beginning to practice
nor end to enlightenment.
There is no beginning to enlightenment
nor end to practice.

Master Dogen

To gain enlightenment,
you must want it as much as a
man whose head is
held under water wants air.

Zen Saying

Just as you see yourself in a mirror,
form and reflection look at each other.
You are not the reflection,
yet the reflection is you.

Tosan

We can achieve nothing.
That is the true meaning of nothingness.

Shunryu Suzuki Roshi

A monk once asked Master Joshu, "Has a dog the Buddha-nature or not?" Joshu said, "Mu!"

Wakuan said, "Why has the foreigner from the West no beard?"

Mumon's Commentary:
Training in Zen has to be real training. Satori has to be real satori. You have to see this foreigner here clearly yourself; then you actually know him. If, however, you talk about "clearly seeing," you have already fallen into dichotomy.

Sakyamuni Holds Up a Flower

Long ago when the World-Honored One was at Mount Grdhrakuta to give a talk, he held up a flower before the assemblage. At this all remained silent. The Venerable Kasho alone broke into a smile. The World-Honored One said, "I have the all-pervading True Dharma, incomparable Nirvana, exquisite teaching of formless form. It does not rely on letters and is transmitted outside scriptures. I now hand it to Maha Kasho."

The wind was flapping a temple flag. Two monks were arguing about it. One said the flag was moving; the other said the wind was moving. Arguing back and forth, they could come to no agreement. The Sixth Patriarch said, "It is neither the wind nor the flag that is moving. It is your mind that is moving." The two monks were struck with awe.

A monk once asked Baso, "What is Buddha?" Baso answered, "No mind, no Buddha."

A teacher of old said, "If the beginning is not right, myriad practices will be useless."

Master Dogen

The Buddha way is under everyone's heel. Immersed in the way, clearly understand right on the spot. Immersed in enlightenment, you yourself are complete. Therefore, even though you arrive at full understanding, still this is only a part of enlightenment. This is how it is with practice throughout the way.

Master Dogen

Thinking is more interesting than knowing, but less interesting than looking.

Johann Wolfgang von Goethe

If all the waves of the Zen stream were alike, innumerable ordinary people would get bogged down.

Zen Saying

Taibai once asked Baso, "What is Buddha?" Baso answered, "Mind is Buddha."

Mumon's Commentary:
If you can at once grasp "it," you are wearing Buddha clothes, eating Buddha food, speaking Buddha words, and living Buddha life; you are a Buddha yourself. Though this may be so, Taibai has misled a number of people and let them trust a scale with a stuck pointer. Don't you now that one

has to rinse out his mouth for three days if he has uttered the word "Buddha"? If he is a real Zen man, he will stop his ears and rush away when he hears "Mind is Buddha."

ZEN NEWS OF THE DAY:
All the News
That's Fit to Hint

Because we enjoy all aspects of life as an unfolding of big mind, we do not care for any excessive joy. So we have imperturbable composure.

Shunryu Suzuki

The Buddha way is, basically, leaping clear of the many and the one; thus there are birth and death, delusion and realization, sentient beings and buddhas.
Yet in attachment blossoms fall, and in aversion weeds spread.

Master Dogen

Zen is not some kind of excitement, but concentration on our usual everyday routine.

Shunryu Suzuki

Seventy-six: done
With this life—
I've not sought heaven,
Don't fear hell.

Fuyo-Dokai (1042–1117)

If there is something you truly want to know, then you truly want to listen to your own wisdom. You know, meditation is learning how to listen with your own wisdom, so that you can see.

Lama Thubten Yeshe

We can enjoy our life only with our limited body.
Without limitation nothing exists.
So we should enjoy our limitations.

Shunryu Suzuki Roshi

Buddhists of the Great Vehicle or Mahayana, to which Zen belongs, believe that one's own experience shows that all objects of perception and thought are not permanent but come into being when other necessary conditions for their existence are fulfilled ... Everything is empty, yet spring comes, flowers bloom, and trees show new growth. Everything is empty, yet even the most ordinary thing is marvelous in itself.

Dr. Miriam Levering

The myriad differences resolved by sitting, all doors opened.
In this still place I follow my nature, be what it may.

Reizan (d. 1411)

Be soft in your practice. Think of the method as a fine silvery
stream, not a raging waterfall.

Sheng-Yen (b. 1931)

Buddha's true dharma body is the "as it is" of empty sky. This empty sky is the "as it is" of buddha's true dharma body.

Master Dogen

For Zen students a weed is a treasure.

Shunryu Suzuki

There are myriads of forms and hundreds of grasses throughout the entire earth, and yet each grass and each form itself is the entire earth.

Master Dogen Zenji

Although your intellect is flying upward, the bird of your conventional notions is feeding below.

Rumi

I thought how sadly beauty of inscape was unknown and buried away from simple people and yet how near at hand it was if they had eyes to see it and it could be called out everywhere again.

Gerard Manley Hopkins (English poet, 1844–89)

Without any intentional, fancy way of adjusting yourself, to express yourself as you are is the most important thing.

Shunryu Suzuki

The Void is fundamentally without spatial dimensions, passions, activities, delusions or right understanding.

Huang Po (d. 850 CE)

When you realize Buddha-dharma, you do not think, "This is realization just as I expected." Even if you think so, realization invariably differs from your expectation.

Master Dogen

Responsibility is to keep the ability to respond.

Robert Duncan (American poet 1919–88)

Nothing prevents us from being natural so much as the desire to appear so.

La Rochefoucauld

Our way is to put the dough in the oven and watch it carefully. Once you know how the dough becomes bread, you will understand enlightenment ...there is no secret in our way.

Shunryu Suzuki

Patience is being patient with patience.
            Sufi Shaykh Junaid (10th century, Baghdad)

For the study of Zen there are three essential require-
ments. The first is a great root of faith; the second is
a great ball of doubt; the third is great tenacity of pur-
pose. A man who lacks any one of these is like a
three-legged kettle with one broken leg.
            Hakuin (1686–1769)

People who know the state of emptiness will always
be able to dissolve their problems by constancy.
            Shunryu Suzuki

DANIEL ABDAL-HAYY MOORE

Born in 1940 in Oakland, California, his first book of poems, *Dawn Visions*, was published by Lawrence Ferlinghetti of City Lights Books, San Francisco, in 1964. He practiced Zen Buddhism with Zen Master Sensei Shunryu Suzuki in San Francisco in the early 1960s, and in 1969 became a Sufi/Muslim, performed the Hajj in 1972, and lived in Morocco, Spain, Algeria, and Nigeria. In 1996 he published *The Ramadan Sonnets*, in 2001 *The Blind Beekeeper*, and in 2005 *The Ecstatic Exchange Series* starting with *Mars & Beyond, Laughing Buddha Weeping Sufi,* and *Salt Prayers*, including a revised version of *Ramadan Sonnets*. He also publishes extensively on the Web, with his own website, www.danielmoorepoetry.com, and at www.deenport.com. He lives with Malika, his wife of twenty-five years, in Philadelphia.

❊

BIBLIOGRAPHY

The Essence of Zen. An anthology of quotations compiled by Maggie Pinkney. Australia: The Five Mile Press, 2005.

Levering, Miriam and Lucian Stryk. *Zen: Images, Texts, and Teachings.* New York: Artisan, 2000.

Moon in a Dewdrop. Writings of Zen Master Dogen, edited by Kazuaki Tanahashi. New York: North Point Press; Farrar, Straus, and Giroux, 1985.

Moore, Daniel. *The Little Box of Zen.* Pennsylvania: Lawrence Teacher Books, 2001.

Stryk, Lucien and Takashi Ikemoto. *The Penguin Book of Zen Poetry.* New York: 1981.

Suzuki, Shunryu. *Zen Mind, Beginner's Mind.* New York and Tokyo: Weatherhill, 1986.

About Cider Mill Press Book Publishers

Good ideas ripen with time. From seed to harvest, Cider Mill Press strives to bring fine reading, information, and entertainment together between the covers of its creatively crafted books. Our Cider Mill bears fruit twice a year, publishing a new crop of titles each Spring and Fall.

Visit us on the web at
www.cidermillpress.com
or write to us at
12 Port Farm Road
Kennebunkport, Maine 04046

*Where Good Books
are Ready for Press*

Other titles in the
Magnetic Wisdom™ Series

Boyfriend Wisdom: Timeouts, Tantrums and Other Tips for Dating Guys Who Act Like Toddlers

MaryJane's FarmGirl Wisdom

Magnetic Quotes and Inspirations

The Secret Life of Girlfriends

Magnetic Quotes and Affirmations

Office Wisdom

Magnetic Quotes and Humor